**BW**

# Fold-Along
# Stories

## Quick & Easy Origami
## Tales For Beginners

text and illustrations by
Christine Petrell Kallevig

**International**
P. O. Box 470505, Cleveland, Ohio 44147

*By the same author*

Folding Stories: Storytelling and Origami Together As One

Holiday Folding Stories: Storytelling and Origami Together For Holiday Fun

All About Pockets: Storytime Activities For Early Childhood

Bible Folding Stories: Old Testament Stories and Paperfolding Together As One

Carry Me Home Cuyahoga: A Children's Historical Novel

Storytime Ink International
P. O. Box 470505, Cleveland, Ohio 44147

ISBN 0-9628769-9-2

Illustrations by Christine Petrell Kallevig
Photographs on page 11 and 39 by Eric Skarl
Photographs on page 15 and 51 by Eleanor Draper
All other photographs by Christine Petrell Kallevig

First Edition
10 9 8 7 6 5 4 3 2 1
Printed in the United States of America

Library of Congress Catalog Card Control Number: 2001-126060

*To the many thousands of students, teachers, parents, and grandparents who have participated so enthusiastically in my paperfolding sessions and storytelling programs since 1990. Thank you for your generous support, contagious energy, and wonderful inspiration. These stories are for you to enjoy and share with others.*

Author Christine Petrell Kallevig sets a friendly tone by testing students on group paperfolding rule number one, "Do what I do." Here she warms them up with silly motions before starting the Fold-Along Story, "The Best Stories." (Directions begin on page 19.)

A brief warm-up activity focuses the group's attention on following directions and allows the storyteller to see that the paper has been distributed properly. It also gives listeners a chance to shift to a better position if their view is obstructed or if they don't have enough space to fold the paper.

Young children are often accustomed to using the floor as a folding surface, but older listeners prefer tables or desks. All of the stories in this book can be folded very successfully without a hard surface to press against as long as the width of the paper is 8.5″ or less.

## The Fold-Along Stories

**TABLE OF CONTENTS**

# How To Make The Origami Figures

1. Origami paper is available in a variety of lovely colors and textures, but all of the figures in this book can be made very satisfactorily with regular 20 lb. office paper. Experiment with different weights, but avoid soft papers that tear easily or resist folding.

2. Many origami figures start as squares, so each side must be exactly the same length. Cut squares from rectangles by folding a corner down and trimming away the excess. This narrow strip of paper can be saved for use in the story on page 19, "The Best Stories."

3. Use a hard, flat surface when making the initial folds on the prefolded model required for each story. Line up edges and corners precisely and hold in place before creasing. This sample model should be as large and as accurate as possible. Use stiff construction paper, freezer wrap, brown paper bags, gift wrap, or art paper to make oversized squares.

4. Follow each step in the order it is given.

5. Explanation of symbols:

   ▸ Shaded areas indicate that the back side of the paper is now facing up.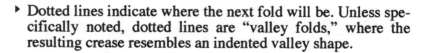

   ▸ Arrows point to the direction of the fold.

   ▸ Dotted lines indicate where the next fold will be. Unless specifically noted, dotted lines are "valley folds," where the resulting crease resembles an indented valley shape.

   ▸ Solid lines mark an existing crease, fold, or edge.

 Dots & dashes mean that the next step is a "mountain fold," where the edges align in the back of the figure and the resulting crease resembles a mountain.

 Flip the figure over to the reverse side.   Rotate the figure.

# Storytelling + Origami = Storigami

Storigami. The concept is simple. While telling a story, you fold paper into various shapes that depict or illustrate the action, setting, or characters. As the story ends, a surprise three-dimensional figure is created. Listeners' minds automatically pair the story events with the progressive folding steps, so while they enjoy the story, they also learn origami, the ancient art of Japanese paperfolding.

I've presented Storigami to the public steadily since 1990. This book, my fourth collection of origami stories, emerged from those performances and features the shortest and easiest stories I tell. They work nicely for all ages in both large and small groups. I tell one or two at the end of programs so that listeners have something tangible to take home, or I use three or more together when teaching origami to beginners.

Success with these simple stories goes a long way toward conquering the irrational fear of origami that's still very prevalent in the general public today. There are also several educational benefits inherent in the combination of the two art forms:

▸ **Improved listening skills:** Paperfolding adds interest and grabs attention. Listeners are curious and motivated to pay closer attention.

▸ **Opportunities to practice right cerebral hemisphere visualization skills:** Listeners imagine the scenes described in the stories and understand the symbolic representations of the progressive origami folds. Researchers believe this ability is related to skills located in the right brain, an area sometimes overlooked in conventional learning tasks.

▸ **Opportunities to practice left cerebral hemisphere language comprehension skills:** Listeners understand the words used in the story. Language comprehension is a skill that is located primarily in the left brain.

▸ **Emphasis is placed on multi-sensory, integrated whole brain learning:** Visual, tactile, and auditory senses are all combined to provide the right and left cerebral hemispheres with input, resulting in an atmosphere of whole-brain learning. Learning is most effective when several areas of the brain are activated simultaneously.

- **Memory enhancement:** Short-term memory is improved through paired associations (story events with folding steps) and multi-sensory stimulation.

- **Improved fine motor skills:** Folding and manipulating paper provides practice in eye-hand coordination.

- **Opportunities to examine and practice spatial relationships:** Spatial concepts include right and left, front and back, top and bottom, inside and outside, beside, under, parallel, symmetrical, etc. These are all key elements of origami.

- **Supplemental material:** The index lists optional follow-up activities in the basic subjects of math, language arts, social studies, art, and science.

- **Opportunities to enhance creativity and social skills:** Increased self-esteem is a by-product of successfully learning new skills and new experiences generate new ideas.

## Who should use Fold-Along Stories?

- Art teachers or origami specialists who need an effective and non-threatening method to teach origami to beginners.

- Language arts teachers, librarians, and storytellers who enjoy audience participation stories or unusual props.

- Recreation, troop, and club leaders who organize and present wholesome activities on limited budgets.

- Camp leaders or program organizers who serve families or groups composed of mixed ages, multiple interests, or diverse ability levels.

- Children and their parents or grandparents who want to build family traditions or participate together in a fun and creative new hobby.

- Activity therapists who are challenged to provide goal-oriented material to diverse populations.

## Guidelines For Best Results:

1. Select stories appropriate for your group.
2. Prefold the origami figure from paper that's large enough to be comfortably seen by all.
3. Be familiar with the story before presenting.
4. Establish structure by explaining rules.
5. Expect and accept imperfect first efforts.
6. Enhance the story with related activities.

**Select carefully:** Every story in this book features a different origami model. The tales can be enjoyed superficially by very young children or may be interpreted on deeper levels by older, more sophisticated listeners. The themes are diverse and even though the origami is easy, there is some variation in folding technique. Use the recommendations on each title page to gauge your group's readiness. The stories were designed as fold-along experiences, but it's perfectly acceptable to simply tell them as is, without asking the audience to participate.

**Prefold before presenting:** When creases are already made, the folding steps fall into place effortlessly and seamlessly, enabling attention to be focused on the needs of the listeners and the dynamics of the story. A flat surface to press against is not needed for refolding, so the sample origami model can be held high for everyone to see. The prefolded crease lines also help clarify where the next folds will be. Even though the sample model does not require creasing as it's refolded, it's best to include the creasing motions anyway. Listeners imitate the presenter, and each step of their paperfolding must be thoroughly creased for best results.

**Try out the story:** Practice refolding the origami model while reading the story aloud so that it's clear which actions or events are represented by the folding steps. Presenting with an open book is acceptable. Memorizing is not necessary.

**Organization diffuses anxiety:** A small percentage of children and adults are so afraid of ruining paper, making mistakes, or attempting new activities that they resist participating. Setting a relaxed, confident tone helps to alleviate these fears. When you're familiar with the story and your origami model is already prefolded, your preparedness reassures everyone. Before distributing paper, provide structure by explaining exactly what you want your listeners to do. Say something like this:

*"There are two rules for group paperfolding that we must all follow. The first is to simply do what I do. Copy my motions. I'll show you exactly what to do. The second rule is just as important. If you are sitting close to someone who seems to be having difficulty doing what I do, please help them. That way, we can all learn together and everyone will easily follow along."*

It's best not to stop and directly assist anyone during the story. Instead, pause and repeat the folding step until everyone has copied you or has been helped by someone else. Offer reassurance that they can do it and that you're not in a hurry. Stopping to give direct help is risky because it can create an undesirable avalanche of dependency. Suddenly, several become unwilling to try and begin demanding special attention, too. This leads to the mistaken impression that paperfolding is difficult, a conclusion that we definitely want to avoid.

**Too much perfection promotes reluctance:** Avoid criticizing lopsided or ragged first results. Instead, emphasize the folding sequence by referring to the progressive steps as they're labeled in the story. To increase quality, suggest making another origami model to share with a friend. Say something like, *"Great job! I knew you could do it! Next time, let's keep the edges lined up while we press the paper. That will make it stand up a little better when it's finished."*

**Broaden the stories with optional activities:** Every story includes suggestions for related discussion topics, creative writing projects, or ways to use or display the origami models. The index also lists themes or subjects addressed in the stories. The activities are not appropriate for all groups and are not designed to be presented together. They are merely intended to spark new ideas for creative applications and enhanced experiences.

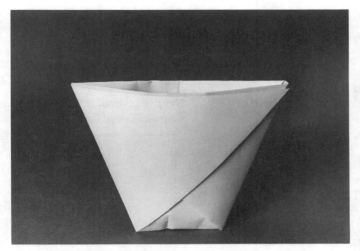

This traditional cup is easy to make and holds water, too.

**About the story:**   An old man reveals how he maintains his strength and good health.

**Recommended ages:**
Listening only: All ages.
Listening & paperfolding: age 4 - adult.

**Required materials:**   A large square prefolded into the cup and then completely unfolded for storytelling.

**Special notes:**
1.  Only the top layer of Step #3 should be folded down. If both layers are folded down, the next step is impossible to fold and there won't be an opening in the cup.

2.  Many folders already know and expect the alternative to Step #3 that's described in item #5 on page 14.

# Three Simple Things

A man with a huge vegetable garden and sprawling fruit trees in his back yard lives in a neighborhood not far from here. He loves to share his produce and gives away much more than he keeps. All the kids call him Mountain Man – not because he's ever lived on a mountain, but because he's as big as a **mountain**, and as old as one, too. *(Demonstrate with Step #1.)*

One day, someone asked him how he managed to live so long and stay so healthy. He said that he tries to do three simple things every day. The first is that he **gives** and **receives** lots and lots of hugs.

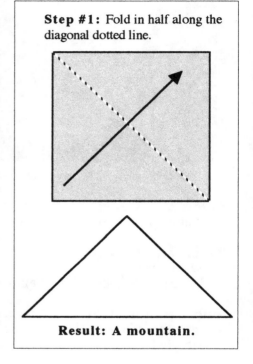

**Step #1:** Fold in half along the diagonal dotted line.

**Result: A mountain.**

*(On the word "gives," fold the first part of Step #2 and on the word "receives," fold the second part.)*

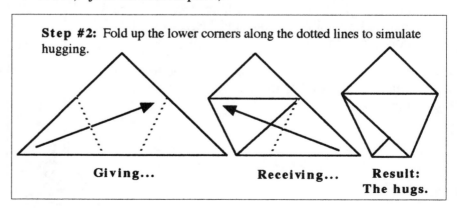

**Step #2:** Fold up the lower corners along the dotted lines to simulate hugging.

Giving...          Receiving...          Result: The hugs.

12

The second thing that he does every day is **lower** his head in thanks for all of his good fortune. *(Demonstrate with Step #3.)*

And the third thing that he does every day, is take a few minutes to sit **back**... *(On the word "back," fold the paper back as shown in Step #4.)*

... and rest as he **drinks** lots and lots of good, pure water. *(Open the completed cup and pretend to drink.)*

Hugging.

Thanking.

Drinking lots of water.

Three simple things. Is a good life really that easy?

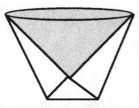

**The complete cup.**

**Step #3:** Fold the top layer down along the dotted line to simulate a lowered head.

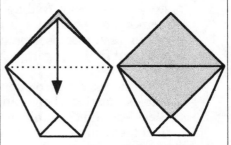

**Result: A lowered head.**

**Step #4:** Mountain fold the remaining layer back along the line as indicated. Push the top corners together slightly to form an opening to the inside.

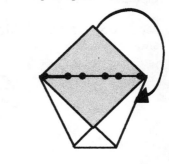

13

# Optional Follow-Up Activities

1. Fold more cups with increasingly smaller squares, making sure to label each step with its name from the story. Pairing story events with folding steps greatly enhances short-term memory of both, and using ever smaller paper decreases rushing and increases precision. One inch squares make tiny cups that fit the fingertips like thimbles.

2. Decorate the finished cup with drawings of fruit trees or vegetables. Predict where your markings will be when unfolded. Were you right? Refold and note when the markings return to final locations.

3. Use the cups as hats for puppets or dolls. A square made from newspaper is large enough to wear. Add streamers, feathers, or flowers for a distinctive style.

4. These cups can function like decorative containers and hold lightweight treats as well as fluids. Make several for party favors or as gifts for special occasions like Mother's Day or Open House.

5. Modify Step #3 by tucking the top layer into the outer fold as shown:

6. "Elijah and the Famine," page 53 from *Bible Folding Stories: Old Testament Stories and Paperfolding Together As One,* uses this same origami model. Compare the techniques used in the two stories. (Bibliographic data is on page 75.)

7. Use this story to introduce or complement discussions about:
   a. Generosity.
   b. Benefits of gardening.
   c. Importance of hydration to good health.
   d. Does love help you live longer?
   e. Gratitude and the responses it promotes in others.

This very easy origami dog face is made in only two steps.

**About the story:** Everyone in town hikes up a mountain to get away from the hot and humid dogs days of summer.

**Recommended ages:**
Listening only: All ages.
Listening & paperfolding: age 4 - adult.

**Required materials:** A dark-colored marking pen and a large square prefolded into the dog and then completely unfolded for storytelling. Do not make the drawings until you tell the story.

**Special notes:**
1. New folders sometimes worry that the shape of their dog ears differs from others. Reassure them that each dog is an unique origami and these individual differences are expected and acceptable.

2. It's optional for listeners to draw the facial features while they fold.

# The Mystery Of Dog Mountain

A couple thousand years ago, the Romans noticed that the weather was often hot and humid whenever the Dog Star, Sirius *(pronounced Sir´- ee-us)*, was high in the night sky. So they called this hot summer weather dog days, after the appearance of the Dog Star.

One summer about 100 years ago, dog days hit real hard in a small town not far from here. It was so hot that everyone started wishing for snow. And then they began dreaming about snow. Before you knew it, no one talked about anything unless it had something to do with snow.

This went on hot day after hot day until finally, everyone in town just had to go and cool off with some real snow. Luckily, they lived close to a tall **mountain** that looked like this.

*(Demonstrate with Step #1.)*

**Snow** covered its whole top, like this. *(Draw the snowcapped mountaintop.)* But this snowy cap was so far away, it took three whole days to hike up to it.

**Step #1:** Fold in half along the diagonal dotted line.

**Result: A tall mountain.**

**Drawing Instructions:**
A. The snowcap
B. The first cave.
C. The second cave.
D. The trail leading to the top.

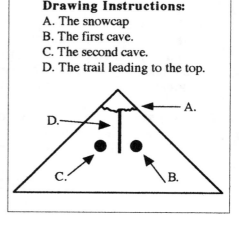

16

The first night, they camped in a **cave** right here. *(Draw a circle to represent the cave.)*

The next night, they camped in another **cave** on the other side of the mountain. *(Draw a circle to represent the other cave.)*

Then they followed a **trail** that led straight up. *(Draw a line up to the top.)* When they finally reached the cold, wet snow on top, they jumped for joy so hard, they set off a terrible earthquake.

When all the rumbling and tumbling stopped, everyone was astonished to see that the mountain had completely changed its shape and split into **three parts** like this. *(Demonstrate with Step #2.)*

From then on, it was called Dog Mountain, but no one remembers why. Can you solve the mystery? Please! Tell me if you know.

*(Invert the figure to reveal the dog face when someone guesses the answer.)*

**Step #2:** Fold the lower corners up along the dotted lines so that the tips end up beyond the figure as shown.

**Result: A changed mountain.**

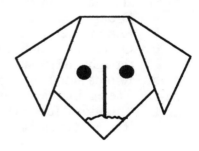

**The complete dog face.**

# Optional Follow-Up Activities

1. Attach a popsicle stick between the two layers to use this little dog as a puppet or cut out the eye holes to make a dog mask. If you construct a dog out of very large paper, you can also wear it as a hat. Organize a parade and wear the masks and hats or wave the puppets.

2. Use the dog as a name tag, bulletin board decoration, ornament, place mark, or lace with yarn for a necklace. Glue tiny dogs onto earring posts or string several together like beaded jewelry.

3. Research the Dog Star, Sirius. How did it get its name? Did ancient Greeks refer to it differently? Draw its constellation. Staple on an origami dog as a three dimensional illustration.

4. Continue the story by writing about what happens the next day. Do the people stay on the mountaintop? Does the hot, humid weather improve? Can they hike down the same way they hiked up? Do they stop thinking about snow? Draw illustrations depicting your creative writing, and then fold the illustrations into dogs during the storytelling.

5. Use this story to introduce or complement discussions about:
   a. Droughts.
   b. Earthquakes.
   c. Obsessive thoughts. The characters were obsessed with thoughts of snow.
   d. Idioms and their origins, such as dog days.
   e. The environmental effects of climate or weather changes.
   f. Traditional folk tales with dogs as main characters.
   g. Roman names for other stars.

These Cleveland kids are proud of their origami hearts.

**About the story:** A storyteller searches for stories that she feels comfortable telling to others.

**Recommended ages:**
Listening only: All ages.
Listening & paperfolding: age 4 - adult.

**Required materials:** A large strip of sturdy construction paper (24″ x 7″ works well for large groups), prefolded into the heart and then completely unfolded for storytelling.

**Special notes:**
1. Some folders have difficulty aligning the top edge to the midline in Step #2. Some attempt to connect the top corners to the middle and others bring the edge over too far or not far enough. Repeat the fold as often as necessary to demonstrate how it is accomplished.

2. Make sure the figure is flipped over to the "house" before folding Step #3.

# The Best Stories

Once there was a storyteller who could only remember **half** the stories she wanted to tell. *(Demonstrate by folding the paper in half as in Step #1.)*

She thought she might be able to remember a **whole** story *(open the paper to its whole length)* if she tried learning just one half at a time. So she studied the first half, **covered** it up, and practiced it out loud. *(On the word, "covered," fold each side of Step #2.)*

Then she studied the second half, **covered** it up, and practiced it out loud, too. She remembered better, but now she felt terribly nervous and afraid when she told the story to other people.

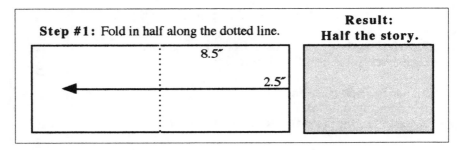

**Step #1:** Fold in half along the dotted line.

**Result: Half the story.**

8.5″

2.5″

**Step #2:** Fold the top edge down along the dotted lines. Flip over to the other side on the word, "house."

**Result: Both halves are hidden.**

Finally the storyteller figured out that there probably wasn't anything wrong with her memory. The real problem was the stories she was trying to tell. They just didn't feel right and they weren't at all the kind of stories that she really believed in.

She decided to leave her **house**...

*(Flip the figure over to the other side to reveal a house.)*

... and search the **four corners** of the world for stories that were more suited to her. *(Demonstrate with Step #3.)*

After traveling to the four corners of the world, *(point to them)* the storyteller visited a tiny library on top of a remote mountain where a wise librarian told her to go home, relax, and look inside herself because that's where her best stories were hiding.

So the storyteller went home to rest, and indeed, when she found her **heart**...

*(Flip the figure over to reveal the complete heart.)*

... she found her stories. And she never had trouble telling them again.

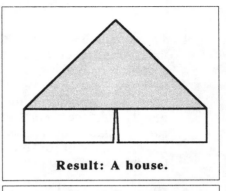

**Result: A house.**

**Step #3:** Fold the 4 corners along the dotted lines. Flip to finish.

1.  2.  3.  4.

**Result: The four corners of the world.**

**The complete heart.**

21

# Optional Follow-Up Activities

1. This simple heart is an ideal way to use the 8.5″ x 2.5″ scraps that are left over when an 8.5″ x 11″ rectangle is cut into a square. Try making more hearts with increasingly smaller strips of paper, making sure to label each step with its name from the story. Pairing story events with folding steps greatly enhances short-term memory of both, and using ever smaller paper decreases rushing and increases precision. Experiment with different dimensions. What size produces the most satisfying results?

2. Write thoughtful or complimentary messages inside the hearts to give as gifts or use as a special occasion cards. Write short poems to exchange on Valentine's Day.

3. Play Pass-the-Heart. After everyone has folded a heart and written their names inside, seat the group in a circle. Pass the hearts from person to person to the rhythm of background music. When the music stops, you must keep the heart you're holding and agree to become that person's secret friend for the rest of the day. Try to be extra thoughtful, complimentary, or kind. At the end of the day, come back together in the circle and guess who had each other's hearts.

4. Identify personality traits, cultural influences, or belief systems that might interfere with your ability or willingness to tell certain stories. Make a list of stories that make you feel uncomfortable. Are there obvious conflicts with your personal characteristics?

5. Adapt the story by substituting other professions for the main character, such as a teacher who couldn't remember her lessons, a minister and her sermons, a musician and her music, a dancer and her choreography, an actor and her lines, a student and her homework, etc.

6. Use this story to introduce or complement discussions about:
   a. Learning styles.
   b. Study habits.
   c. Importance of knowing yourself and your own values.
   d. Meditation.

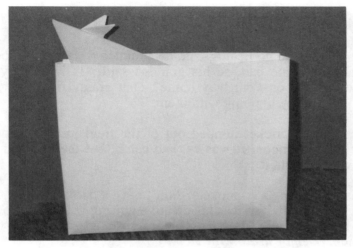

This practical pocket is constructed in three easy steps.

**About the story:** A boy needs a container for his crickets, so he invents a paper pocket.

**Recommended ages:**
    Listening only: All ages.
    Listening & paperfolding: age 4 - adult.

**Required materials:** A large rectangle prefolded into the pocket and then completely unfolded for storytelling.

**Special notes:**
1. The figure must be flipped to the reverse side before folding Step #2.

2. Very young folders often have difficulty making straight creases. Encourage them to take their time. Then show them how to line up the edges and press a finger all the way along the fold to make it lay flat.

# The Mother Of Invention

Melvin planned to go fishing with his grandpa right after school. But they needed some bait, so his grandpa said, "Why don't you catch some crickets on your way home? That grassy field next to your school is usually hopping with them."

Sure enough, a cricket jumped out of the field just as Melvin walked by that afternoon. It was easy to catch, but then he had to figure out where to put it.

He wasn't wearing any pockets, didn't have a book bag, and the only thing he had with him was his creative writing notebook. So he tore out a blank page, **folded up the bottom edge**, and put the cricket inside. *(Demonstrate with Step #1.)*

The little critter squeezed out quicker than he could spell escape, so he solved the problem by **closing both sides**, like this. *(Demonstrate with Step #2.)*

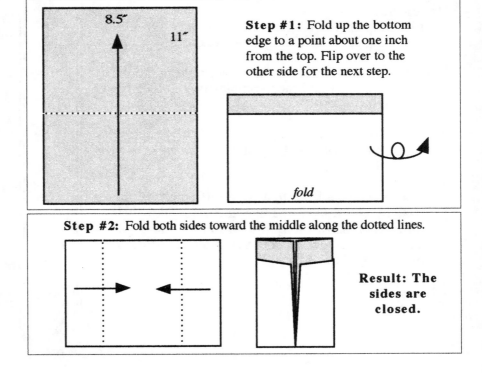

**Step #1:** Fold up the bottom edge to a point about one inch from the top. Flip over to the other side for the next step.

*fold*

**Step #2:** Fold both sides toward the middle along the dotted lines.

**Result: The sides are closed.**

That worked better, except the sides kept popping up whenever Melvin added another cricket. *(Hold the figure so that the last folds stand upright.)*

So he pressed the **top edge down** to keep the sides sealed nice and tight, like this. *(Demonstrate with Step #3.)*

Melvin caught six crickets by the time he got home. His grandpa was waiting for him down by the pond and was just as happy to see his paper pocket as he was to see the crickets.

He patted his shoulder and said, "Grandson, today you proved that necessity is the mother of invention. And just in time, too, because the mother of an inventor, your mama, wants fish for supper, so we'd better get busy and catch her some!"

**Step #3:** Fold the top layer down along the dotted line and flip the figure over to the reverse side to reveal the complete pocket. Squeeze the sides slightly together to create an opening in the top. Insert your fingers to simulate capturing the crickets.

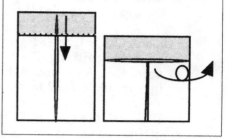

**The complete pocket.**

25

# Optional Follow-Up Activities

1. This simple origami pocket can be constructed from rectangles of any size or dimension, including squares. Try folding another pocket with a different size piece of paper, making sure to label each step with its action from the story. Pairing the story events with the folding steps greatly enhances short-term memory of both. Don't be surprised when individual folders produce pockets with slightly different dimensions. The size of the pocket is determined by the width of the top layer that's folded down in Step #3.

2. Decorate a finished pocket with drawings about catching crickets or fishing. Predict where your pictures will be when unfolded. Were you right? Refold and note when the drawings return to final locations.

3. Research the origin of the proverb, "Necessity is the mother of invention." It appears in the dialogue *Republic,* by the ancient Greek philosopher, Plato. What was the original context?

4. These pockets can function as throw-away containers for nuisance items like the shells of sunflower or pumpkin seeds. They can also hold lightweight treats or messages. Make several for party favors or as gifts for special occasions like Mother's Day or Open House.

5. "Penny's Paper Pocket," p. 40 in *All About Pockets: Storytime Activities for Early Childhood,* uses this same origami model. Compare the techniques used in the two stories. Use the paper pockets as props for other activities suggested in the book. (Bibliographic data is on p. 75.)

6. Use this story to introduce or complement discussions about:
   a. Problem solving.
   b. Fishing.
   c. Importance of grandparents in the lives of children.
   d. Proverbs and their meanings.
   e. History of pockets.
   f. Crickets, their habitats and usefulness to humans.

Make this crown out of newspaper to be large enough to wear.

**About the story:** A girl celebrates her birthday with her favorite flowers and a surprise companion.

**Recommended ages:**
Listening only: All ages.
Listening & paperfolding: age 5 - adult.

**Required materials:** A large tablet or chalkboard for recording answers and a large square, prefolded into the crown, and then completely unfolded for storytelling.

**Special notes:**
1. In Step #3, some folders try to fold the loose tips so that they connect to the bottom point rather than jut out beyond it. Show them the prefolded crease line on your model as an example.

2. The crown will separate if the crease in Step #4 is not pressed firmly.

27

# Queen For A Day

This story is partially improvised and is different each time it's told. Ask the listeners to provide the following facts before you begin telling the story. Display them during the story.

1. A girl's name.
2. A number between one and ninety.
3. The name of a city.
4. A number between one and twelve.
5. A favorite flower.
6. An animal.

Not long ago, a girl named _____ *(the answer to question #1)* celebrated her _____ *(the answer to question #2)* birthday. She lived in _____ *(the answer to question #3)* where it was the custom to give every birthday girl fresh flowers as soon as she woke up.

_____*(Name)*_____ opened her eyes at _____ o'clock *(the answer to question #4)* and the first thing she saw was a vase full of _____ *(the answer to question #5)*.

She wanted to carry them with her all day, so she placed some of them into a **satchel**, that looked like this. *(Fold Step #1. Then pretend to add flowers inside.)*

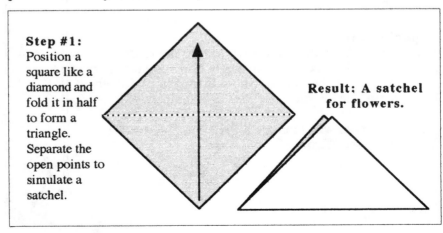

**Step #1:**
Position a square like a diamond and fold it in half to form a triangle. Separate the open points to simulate a satchel.

**Result: A satchel for flowers.**

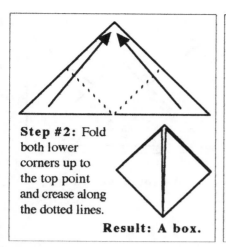

**Step #2:** Fold both lower corners up to the top point and crease along the dotted lines.

**Result: A box.**

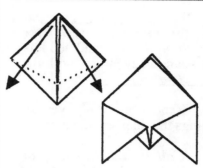

**Step #3:** Fold both tips down and crease along the dotted lines to simulate the opening of the box.

The next thing ___(Name)___ noticed was a big **box**, that looked like this. *(Demonstrate with Step #2.)*

She **opened** it, *(demonstrate with Step #3)*

...folded **down** its lid, *(demonstrate with Step #4)*

...and then looked **inside**. *(Demonstrate with Step #5.)*

She was shocked to see a big, scary _____ *(the answer to question #6).*

It curled its lips into a goofy grin, gave her a big wet kiss, and shouted, "Happy birthday, baby! Here's something special for you to wear all day long. And not only that! You can do whatever you want until twelve o'clock tonight!"

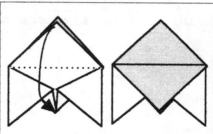

**Step #4:** Fold only the top layer down to the lower point and crease along the dotted line to simulate folding down the lid of the box.

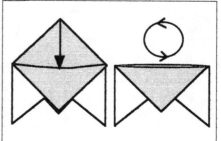

**Step #5:** Stuff the top point into the inside of the crown to simulate looking inside the box.

So ___(Name)___ put on the **crown** *(invert the result of Step #5)* and had lots of strange adventures with the ___(Animal)___.

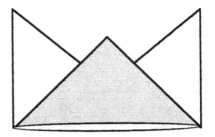

**The complete crown.**

Some of the weirder things that happened were:

*(Call on the listeners for suggestions. In the unlikely event that they don't have any ideas, make up a few of your own, the wackier, the better.)*

Yes, ___(Name)___ had a wonderful birthday. And isn't it amazing what you can get away with when you're wearing a crown?

# Optional Follow-Up Activities

1. This traditional origami crown can be constructed from squares of any size. Crowns made from 2″ squares will fit a fingertip and 20″ squares can be worn like a hat. Try folding miniature crowns, making sure to label each step with its name from the story. Pairing story events with folding steps greatly enhances short-term memory of both, and using ever smaller paper decreases rushing and increases precision. The points of the crown may differ each time according to the folding angle in Step #3.

2. Make shiny crowns from aluminum foil. Use a pencil to etch in textures or decorations.

3. Fold back the middle point and adjust the lower corners to make a variety of animal faces. Here are some examples. The first is simply a kitty face added to the crown with the middle point folded back. The rabbit ears in the second are made by folding the lower corners to the back. The third folds down the rabbit ears to make a pig or cow face. Experiment with other adjustments. Use your imagination to make more.

4. Make a tropical fish by adding the following steps:

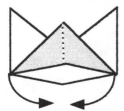 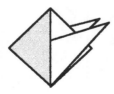 

Open the crown and push the opposite corners together as shown above. A fold will form on the dotted line as it collapses together. Flatten into a diamond shape, then simply fold the lower edge up on both sides to form pectoral fins.

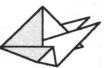

**The complete fish.**

5. Decorate a finished crown. Add feathers or paper jewels. Then create a fictional kingdom where the crown owner resides. Describe it and write a story about something unusual that happens there. Staple the origami crown to the story as a three-dimensional illustration.

6. Practice other forms of improvised stories. Structure with preset answers or ask for audience responses as the tale progresses. Try passing a crown throughout a group. The person holding the crown adds a sentence or scene to a story-in-progress. Guide the direction of the plot by providing a setting or characters, or make a rule that the tale must end with the last person.

7. Use this story to introduce or complement discussions about:
   a. Cultural vs. individual birthday traditions.
   b. How it feels to be celebrated.
   c. Different species of flowers.
   d. Improvisation in other areas, such as drama, music or the visual arts.
   e. Is there a place for crowns and royalty in our modern world?

This free-standing fox is four layers thick.

**About the story:**  A fox is trapped and relocated after stealing eggs and chickens from nearby farms.

**Recommended ages:**
Listening only: All ages.
Listening & paperfolding: age 6 - adult.

**Required materials:**  Use the largest square you can find, prefolded into the fox and then completely unfolded for storytelling.

**Special notes:**
1. Step #3 must be a mountain fold, not a valley fold like most of the others in this book. Emphasize that the points connect in the back of the figure, not the front.

2. Make sure the figure is positioned so that the loose tips (which become the ears) are pointing up before folding Step #4.

# Here Today Gone Tomorrow

The farms near **Rainbow Mountain** *(demonstrate with Step #1)* were missing eggs and chickens every night.

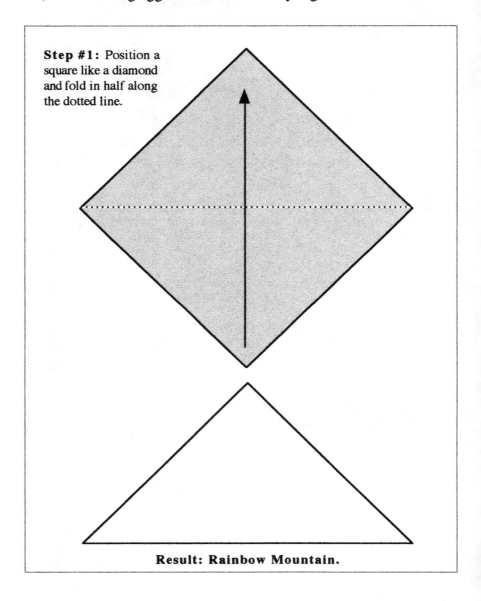

**Step #1:** Position a square like a diamond and fold in half along the dotted line.

**Result: Rainbow Mountain.**

Fox prints were always left behind at the scene of the crime, so a trapper was hired to capture the thief and move it somewhere else. The greedy fox was easily lured into a big **box** full of eggs. *(Demonstrate with Step #2.)*

Then the trapper drove to a **remote mountain** that didn't have any farms or neighborhoods near it at all. *(Demonstrate with Step #3.)*

He **cracked** open the box, *(demonstrate with Step #4)*

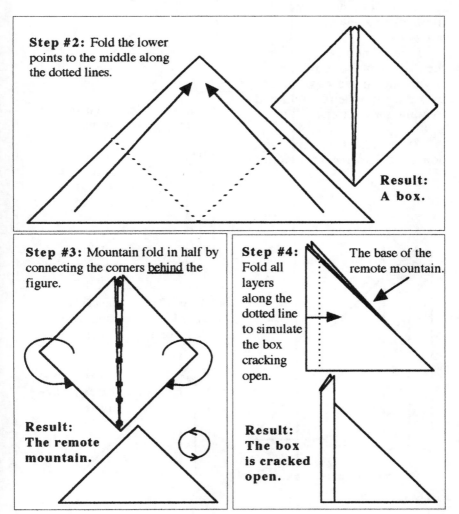

**Step #2:** Fold the lower points to the middle along the dotted lines.

**Result: A box.**

**Step #3:** Mountain fold in half by connecting the corners <u>behind</u> the figure.

**Result: The remote mountain.**

**Step #4:** Fold all layers along the dotted line to simulate the box cracking open.

The base of the remote mountain.

**Result: The box is cracked open.**

... and out popped the **fox**. *(Demonstrate with Step #5.)*

The fox shook his **head**, *(demonstrate with Step #6)*

... twitched his tail **back and forth**, *(demonstrate with Step #7)*

... and sat down to watch the trapper drive away.

Forewarned is forearmed, the sly fox thought. He'd never put all his eggs in one basket again when he returned to home sweet home.

After all, if at first you don't succeed, try, try again.

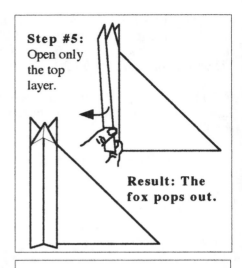

**Step #5:** Open only the top layer.

**Result: The fox pops out.**

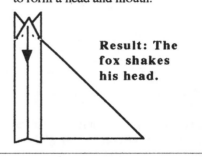

**Step #6:** Fold down both layers to form a head and mouth.

**Result: The fox shakes his head.**

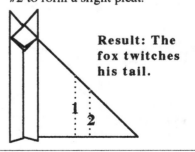

**Step #7:** Fold the tail back on line #1 and then forward on line #2 to form a slight pleat.

**Result: The fox twitches his tail.**

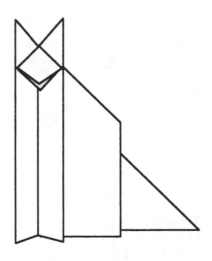

**The complete fox.**

# Optional Follow-Up Activities

1.  Make more foxes with increasingly smaller squares, making sure to label each step with its name from the story. Pairing story events with folding steps greatly enhances short-term memory of both, and using ever smaller paper decreases rushing and increases precision. Because this model is so dense, very small figures may require tweezers or pliers to crease through all the layers in Step #4.

2.  There's another Storigami about Rainbow Mountain and Sly Fox on page 57 in *Holiday Folding Stories: Storytelling and Origami Together for Holiday Fun.* Tell the two stories. Compare and contrast the folding methods. (Bibliographic data is on page 75.)

3.  Use the fox origami as a puppet for other stories or fables, or as name tags, bulletin board decorations, ornaments, place marks, or lace with yarn for necklaces. Glue tiny foxes onto earring posts or string several together like beaded jewelry.

4.  Modify the ears to make a dog. Fold up the tip of the tail to create a tail-wagging effect.

5.  Draw details like fur and eyes on the finished models. Predict where your markings will be when unfolded. Were you right? Refold and note when the markings return to final locations.

6.  Continue the story by writing about what happens to the fox as he finds his way back to Rainbow Mountain. How long does it take? Does he discover other farms to raid or does he give up on stealing eggs and chickens in order to eat more natural foods? Draw illustrations for your creative writing and then add an origami fox.

7. Several fables, legends, and folk tales feature foxes as prominent characters. Identify as many as you can. Do the stories share similar themes or plots? Is the fox always a scoundrel? What traits does a fox possess naturally that contribute to its fiendish reputation?

8. Experiment with different paper textures, such as aluminum foil, construction paper, waxed paper, freezer wrap, paper grocery bags, gift wrap, or wallpaper. Avoid tissue papers or plastics that do not retain creases.

9. There are five common proverbs in this story. Research other proverbs and include as many as possible in your own folding story with this origami fox or other models featured in this book.

10. Use this story to introduce or complement discussions about:
    a.  Stealing.
    b.  Does the punishment (banishment) fit the crime?
    c.  Is punishment effective or does it simply teach the criminal how to be more cunning in future efforts?
    d.  The natural habitats of foxes. Are they disappearing?
    e.  The use of proverbs in folk tales and fables.

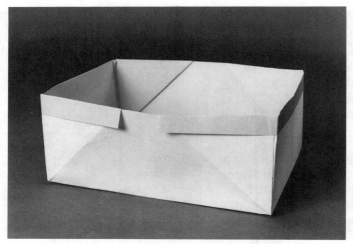

This handy box is easy to make and has practical uses, too.

**About the story:** Shy Turtle hides beneath the water of his pond until a long drought forces him to reveal himself.

**Recommended ages:**
Listening only: All ages.
Listening & paperfolding: age 6 - adult.

**Required materials:** A large rectangle prefolded into the box and then completely unfolded for storytelling.

**Special notes:**
1. On Step #4, make sure the four corners fit <u>under</u> the narrow band.

2. Folders sometimes worry that the paper will tear or fall apart when they try to open the box in the last step. Reassure them and then show them how to define the final shape of the box by pinching and sharpening each of the corners.

# Shy Turtle Comes Out Of His Shell

Shy Turtle lived in a **pond** that looked something like this. *(Hold up a rectangle to represent the pond, as shown to the right.)*

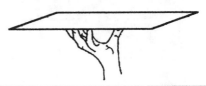

He was very private and always hid beneath the water whenever visitors showed up. The only part of Shy Turtle that anyone ever saw was his large **mouth** that snapped shut and slowly opened again, like this. *(Demonstrate by closing Step #1 in a snapping motion and then opening it again very slowly.)*

Since he never let any other part of himself be seen, people always said, "Look! There's a turtle's mouth. I wonder what kind it is?" Their curiosity made him feel special and mysterious as he sneakily snapped at flies and mosquitoes all day and most of the night.

But then the weather got hot and dry. Weeks passed without any rain and the pond began to dry up, shrinking **smaller** and **smaller**, like this.

*(Fold one side of Step #2 each time you say the word, "smaller.")*

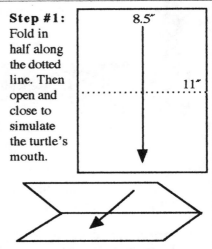

**Step #1:** Fold in half along the dotted line. Then open and close to simulate the turtle's mouth.

8.5″

11″

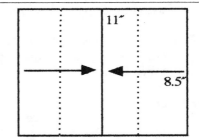

11″

8.5″

**Step #2:** Open Step #1 and fold the sides to the middle along the dotted lines, simulating a shrinking pond.

**Result: A smaller pond.**

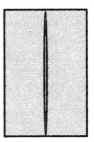

The drought lasted so long, Shy Turtle's pond changed into a narrow **creek** with steep banks, like this. *(Demonstrate with Step #3.)*

Now there wasn't enough water to hide under, so Shy Turtle folded each of his four feet into his protective shell. First he folded in his **front feet**. *(Demonstrate with the top two corners of Step #4.)*

Then he folded in his **back feet**, too. *(Fold the bottom corners of Step #4.)*

**Step #3:** Fold the loose edges about 1/2 inch back along the dotted lines to simulate steep banks along a creek bed.

**Result: A narrow creek.**

Finally the last drop of pond water evaporated, so Shy Turtle panicked and tucked his **head** and **tail** inside, too. *(On the word, "head," fold down the top edge of Step #5. Fold up the bottom edge on the word, "tail.")*

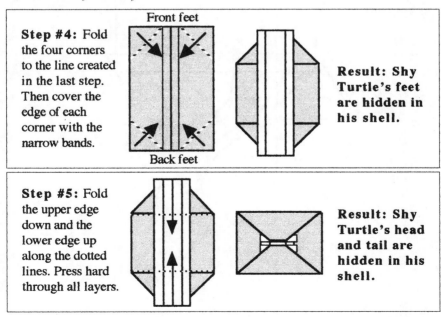

**Step #4:** Fold the four corners to the line created in the last step. Then cover the edge of each corner with the narrow bands.

Front feet

Back feet

**Result: Shy Turtle's feet are hidden in his shell.**

**Step #5:** Fold the upper edge down and the lower edge up along the dotted lines. Press hard through all layers.

**Result: Shy Turtle's head and tail are hidden in his shell.**

He stayed hidden inside his shell for a long time, hoping that a big downpour would fill his pond again. But when his skin began to dry up, he knew he had to come out of his shell and find a new place to live. Shy Turtle **stretched**, *(on the word, "stretched," open the box, as in Step #6)*

... and then **flipped** himself over, *(invert the box, as shown below)*

... for the first time, revealing exactly what kind of turtle he was. A box turtle!

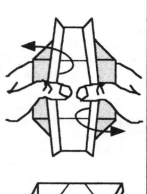

**Step #6:**
Unfold the last step, then insert your thumbs into the opening and gently pull the right and left sides apart. It will open into a box. Pinch the corners and bottom edges to sharpen and define its shape.

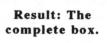

**Result: The complete box.**

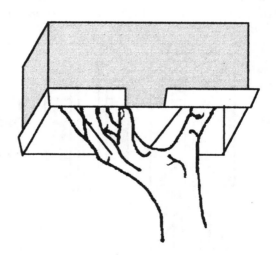

# Optional Follow-Up Activities

1. This traditional origami box can be constructed from rectangles of any size or dimension, including squares. Fold another box with a different size piece of paper, making sure to label each step with its name from the story. Pairing the story events with the folding steps greatly enhances short-term memory of both. Don't be surprised when individual folders produce boxes with slightly different dimensions. The size of the box is determined by the width of the narrow bands (the steep banks of the creek) in Step #3.

2. Box lids are created by slightly increasing the width of the narrow bands in Step #3. The directions suggest that the bands be 1/2″ wide. If you increase the width of the band to 3/4″ in a second box, it will be slightly larger and fit snugly over the top of the first box.

3. Make long shallow boxes by creasing Step #1 on its 11″ midline rather than along its 8.5″ midline. All other steps remain the same.

4. Decorate a finished box with turtle shell designs. Then make similar designs on another unfolded piece of paper. Fold the decorated paper into a box. Compare it to the first box. How are they different? How are they alike? Decide if it's more efficient to decorate paper before folding, or after. Does it matter which side is facing up when you begin? Experiment with different starting positions.

5. Use these boxes to store other origami models or make boxes as gifts, to contain gifts, or as throw-away containers for nuisance items like the shells of sunflower seeds.

6. Experiment with different paper textures, such as aluminum foil, construction paper, waxed paper, freezer wrap, paper grocery bags, gift wrap, or wallpaper. Avoid tissue papers or plastics that do not retain creases.

7. Continue the story by writing about what happens to Shy Turtle during his move and at his new home. How far does he travel? Does he make any friends? Does the dry weather

improve? Draw illustrations depicting your creative writing, and then fold the illustrations into boxes. If you start Step #1 with the illustrations facing up, they will be framed by the sides of the box when folded.

8. Use this story to introduce or complement discussions about:
   a. Overcoming shyness.
   b. How it feels to be shy.
   c. Shy Turtle enjoyed feeling mysterious. Does being shy have rewards? Special privileges?
   d. Identifying different species of turtles and their habitats.
   e. The environmental effects of climate or weather changes.
   f. Traditional folk tales with turtles as main characters.

One square cut into two triangles produces two mice.

**About the story:** A hound dog longs to share his retirement with someone who appreciates peace and quiet as much as he does.

**Recommended ages:**
Listening only: All ages.
Listening & paperfolding: age 7 - adult.

**Required materials:** A large square cut in half along its diagonal midline, resulting in two large right triangles. Prefold one triangle into the mouse, and then completely unfold for storytelling. If you prefer not to cut the square, simply fold it in half to form the triangle required in Step #1. The resulting mouse will be bulkier.

**Special notes:**
1. In Steps #4 and #5, some folders try to fold the corners to the middle, instead of the sides to the middle. Emphasize the correct folding method by sliding your finger along the whole length of the edge before folding.

2. The figure must be flipped over before proceeding with Step #5.

# Silence Is Golden

Once there was an old hound dog who had long, **droopy ears** that looked like this. *(Demonstrate with Step #1.)*

He served his master well throughout his whole life, and now that he could no longer hunt, he planned to spend the rest of his days lounging in the lush grass down by the pond. He didn't like to be disturbed, so he often blocked out all sounds by letting his long ears **fold over**, like this. *(Demonstrate with Step #2.)*

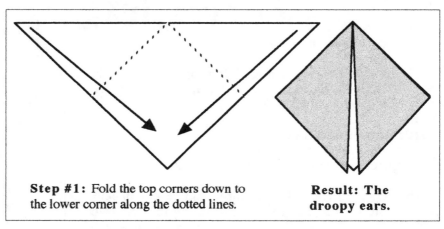

**Step #1:** Fold the top corners down to the lower corner along the dotted lines.

**Result: The droopy ears.**

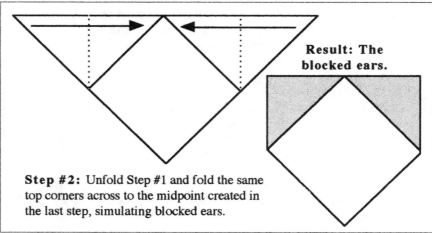

**Result: The blocked ears.**

**Step #2:** Unfold Step #1 and fold the same top corners across to the midpoint created in the last step, simulating blocked ears.

Not even the penetrating howl of his old enemy, **Sly Fox**, *(demonstrate with Step #3)* could be heard when his ears were folded over.

The silence helped him see things that he'd never noticed before, like the **butterflies** that hovered over the sweet, pink clover *(demonstrate with Step #4)* and the **mosquitoes** that tried, but failed, to drill through his tough skin. *(Demonstrate with Step #5.)*

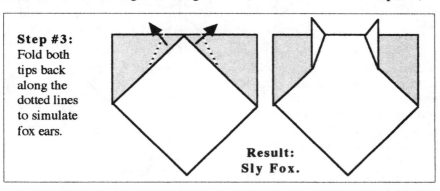

**Step #3:** Fold both tips back along the dotted lines to simulate fox ears.

**Result: Sly Fox.**

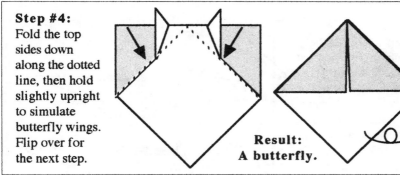

**Step #4:** Fold the top sides down along the dotted line, then hold slightly upright to simulate butterfly wings. Flip over for the next step.

**Result: A butterfly.**

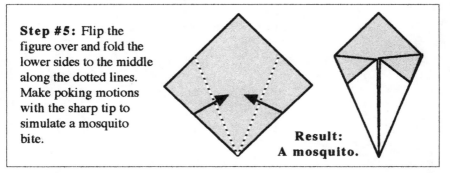

**Step #5:** Flip the figure over and fold the lower sides to the middle along the dotted lines. Make poking motions with the sharp tip to simulate a mosquito bite.

**Result: A mosquito.**

He studied the pond, too. He loved to watch the **tadpoles** *(demonstrate with Step #6)* wiggle so skillfully between the rocks. They were his best friends until they suddenly changed into rude, croaky frogs who plopped on his nose whenever he tried to nap.

The hound dog longed to spend his long, lazy days with someone who enjoyed peace and quiet as much as he did. Finally his wish came true. Can you guess the identity of his new, quiet friend?

*(Hold up the result of Step #7, the complete mouse.)*

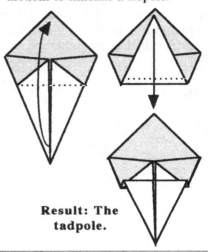

**Step #6:** Fold the lower point up to the top, then fold it back to create a slight pleat. Make swimming motions to simulate a tadpole.

**Result: The tadpole.**

**Step #7:** Fold the figure in half and rotate it so that the ears pop straight up. Shape the body by folding under the bottom edge on both sides, as shown.

**Result: The complete mouse.**

# Optional Follow-Up Activities

1. This traditional origami mouse can be constructed from right triangles of any size, as long as the two perpendicular sides are of equal length. Try folding miniature mice, making sure to label each step with its name from the story. Pairing story events with folding steps greatly enhances short-term memory of both, and using ever smaller paper decreases rushing and increases precision.

2. Make jewelry out of the tiny origami mice by gluing them to earrings or stringing several together with thread. Use colorful papers and beads for variety and contrast.

3. Organize Storigami presentations according to the skills mastered in each story. For example, an excellent warm-up origami for this mouse is the heart on pages 19-22. It introduces side-to-the-middle folding and corner folding that are required in this model. The bird featured in the next story (pages 51-56) reinforces many of the same techniques, but also adds a simple reverse fold, which is enhanced further in the origami car (pages 63-69). When folders are comfortable with these basic techniques, they're better prepared to follow standard origami directions on their own.

4. Investigate directions for constructing other origami mice. Mice are popular models and several versions are available in easy origami books or on the Internet. Origami books are usually shelved in the 736 section (Dewey decimal system) of public libraries.

5. Do people really notice more details when their sense of hearing is limited as was the case in this story? Divide into two groups that have the same average ages and equal numbers of males and females. One is the control group, the other has plugged ears. Place both groups in the same setting, either outside or in an unfamiliar room, and ask each person to write down everything he sees in ten minutes. Compare results. Did other factors, such as varying eyesight, spelling, or handwriting skills influence the outcome? How could the experiment be improved to eliminate these factors?

6. Use these mice as props or puppets for other fables, plays, or folk tales that feature mice as main characters.

7. Is this origami mouse perfectly symmetrical? Analyze each step. Do they produce exactly the same dimensions on all sides, or just to the right and left?

8. Decorate a finished mouse or a family of mice. Give them names and describe their personalities. Then ask yourself what unusual or humorous event might happen around these characters. Describe it and then resolve any conflicts arising from this situation. Staple the origami mice to the final draft as three-dimensional illustrations.

9. Use this story to introduce or complement discussions about:
   a. The literal and symbolic meanings for the proverbial title, "Silence is Golden."
   b. Life style changes relating to aging.
   c. Retirement options. Which are best and why?
   d. Individual tolerance for noise and/or activity.
   e. Life cycles of amphibians.

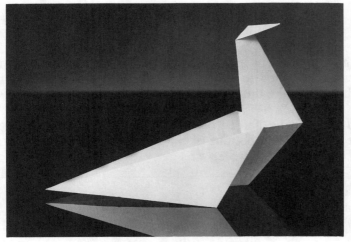

This elegant bird is folded in seven easy steps.

**About the story:** A boy crashes his new sled, then turns it into something that flies even better down the hill.

**Recommended ages:**
Listening only: All ages.
Listening & paperfolding: age 7 - adult.

**Required materials:** A large square prefolded into the bird and then completely unfolded for storytelling.

**Special notes:**
1. Sometimes folders try to fold the corners to the middle instead of the sides in Steps #2 and #3.

2. Step #4 and #5 <u>must</u> be mountain folds, not valley folds like most of the others in this book. Emphasize that the points and corners connect in the back of the figure, not the front.

3. Folders must continue to grip the lower corner as they pull down the inside point of Step #6. The figure will separate if they release that corner.

51

# The New Sled

Once there was a boy named Jeremy. Winter was his favorite season because he loved to slide down the long, **steep hill** in his backyard. It looked like this. *(Demonstrate with Step #1.)*

He had fun, but he had to be careful, too, because there were some **pine trees** at the bottom of the hill. The tallest one looked like this. *(Demonstrate with Step #2.)*

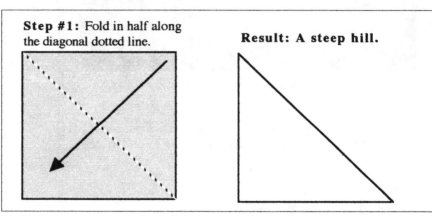

**Step #1:** Fold in half along the diagonal dotted line.

**Result: A steep hill.**

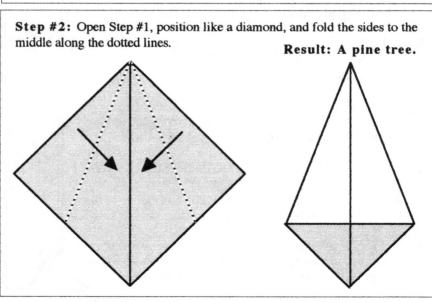

**Step #2:** Open Step #1, position like a diamond, and fold the sides to the middle along the dotted lines.

**Result: A pine tree.**

One winter, Jeremy got a new **sled** as a birthday present. *(Demonstrate with Step #3.)* It was built long and narrow for extra speed and had sloping sides on one end where he could tuck his legs for extra protection.

He practiced steering by sliding partway down the hill. Then he climbed all the way to the top and pushed off for what he hoped would be the fastest, most exciting ride he'd ever had.

It was fast! And exciting! But so much snow blew back in his face, he couldn't see where he was going. He panicked and rolled off just as the sled crashed full speed into one of those pine trees at the bottom of the hill.

Jeremy was okay, but his new sled **bent in half**, like this. *(Demonstrate with Step #4.)*

When he tugged it out of the trees, it **bent in half** again, like this. *(Demonstrate with Step #5.)*

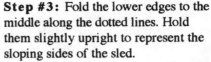

**Step #3:** Fold the lower edges to the middle along the dotted lines. Hold them slightly upright to represent the sloping sides of the sled.

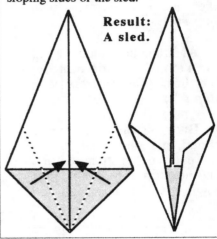

**Result: A sled.**

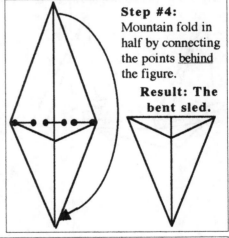

**Step #4:** Mountain fold in half by connecting the points <u>behind</u> the figure.

**Result: The bent sled.**

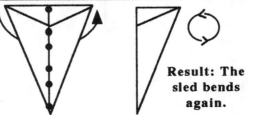

**Step #5:** Mountain fold in half by connecting the top corners <u>behind</u> the figure. Then turn upside down for the next step.

**Result: The sled bends again.**

As Jeremy was trying to figure out how to lug it home, he reached inside and pulled out a **long pointy piece**, like this. (*Demonstrate with Step #6.*)

And then he folded the top down to make a little **handle**, like this. (*Demonstrate with Step #7.*)

But instead of being ruined, his new sled turned out even better than before. The next time, he really flew down the hill. Can you see why?

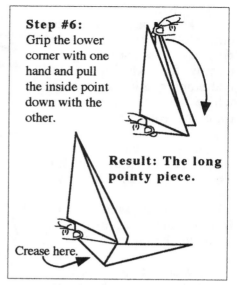

**Step #6:** Grip the lower corner with one hand and pull the inside point down with the other.

**Result: The long pointy piece.**

Crease here.

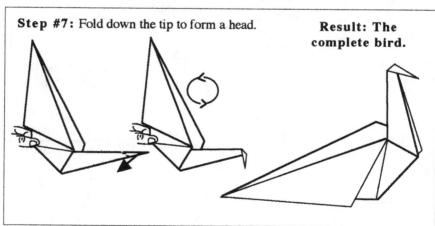

**Step #7:** Fold down the tip to form a head.

**Result: The complete bird.**

# Optional Follow-Up Activities

1. Make more birds with increasingly smaller squares, making sure to label each step with its name from the story. Pairing story events with folding steps greatly enhances short-term memory of both, and using ever smaller paper decreases rushing and increases precision.

2. Draw details like feathers and eyes on the finished models. Predict where your markings will be when unfolded. Were you right? Refold and note when the markings return to final locations.

3. Use the birds as name tags, bulletin board decorations, ornaments, place marks, or lace with yarn for necklaces. Glue tiny birds onto earring posts or string several together like beaded jewelry.

4. These birds can function like decorative containers and hold lightweight treats inside the body. Make several for party favors or as gifts for special occasions like Mother's Day or Open House.

5. Study the concept of proportion by making a family of birds. Cut 16 squares, each square progressively 1/2″ smaller, starting with 8.5″ per side and ending with 1″ per side. Distribute to several folders. When each bird is complete, measure it from the tip of its tail to the corner of its breast bone. Graph the results.

6. Experiment with different paper textures, such as aluminum foil, construction paper, waxed paper, freezer wrap, paper grocery bags, gift wrap, or wallpaper. Avoid tissue papers or plastics that do not retain creases.

7. Will these birds fly? Will they float? Conduct experiments. Test birds constructed out of various papers. Analyze the design elements that enable or prohibit flying or floating. Modify the birds to correct the problems.

8. Research the prevalence of sledding accidents. How many injuries are reported each year? What kind of injuries are most common? Who gets hurt most often? Were there any fatalities? Is there someone who has personal experience

with sledding injuries within the group? Review basic safety rules. What rules did Jeremy violate? Would he have been safer sledding with a partner?

9. Use this model to illustrate the concept of symmetry. Most folding steps for the bird are symmetrical. Two are not. Identify which are asymmetrical.

10. Use this story to introduce or complement discussions about:
    a. Winter sports.
    b. Winter safety.
    c. Creative problem solving.
    d. Different types of origami birds.

This traditional piano is constructed in only six steps.

**About the story:** Mrs. Ivory finds exactly what she's looking for on the clearance table at the music store.

**Recommended ages:**
Listening only: All ages.
Listening & paperfolding: age 7 - adult.

**Required materials:** A large square prefolded into the piano and then completely unfolded for storytelling.

**Special notes:**
1. Make sure the folded edge is positioned on top in Steps #2 and #3.

2. Step #5 must be pressed firmly through all layers in order for the keyboard to retain its shape. Some folders try to roll the front flap up instead of creasing each step firmly.

# The Perfect Bargain

Once there was a piano teacher named Mrs. Ivory. She had many students. Some couldn't pay for lessons, but she taught them anyway because she wanted everyone to love music as much as she did. Sometimes she had trouble paying her bills, too, so she often looked for bargains in the **newspaper**. *(Demonstrate with Step #1.)*

Mrs. Ivory loved to find things for sale at **half** their regular price.

*(On the word "half," fold the figure in half, as in Step #2.)*

**Step #1:** Fold in half along the dotted line. Then open to simulate a newspaper.

**Result: A newspaper.**

Once she was asked to play the piano at a fancy dinner, but she couldn't decide what to play. She **opened** *(unfold Step #2)* and **closed** *(on the word "closed," fold Step #3)* all her music books, but nothing seemed right for this very special event.

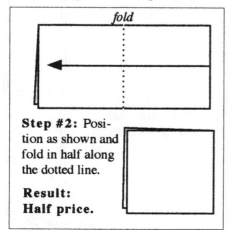

**Step #2:** Position as shown and fold in half along the dotted line.
**Result: Half price.**

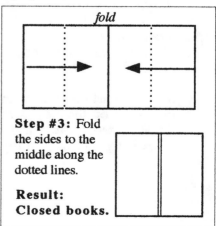

**Step #3:** Fold the sides to the middle along the dotted lines.
**Result: Closed books.**

**Step #4:** Insert your thumb between the first and second layers, then swing the top layer over to the right. Crease the resulting triangle. Repeat on the other side.

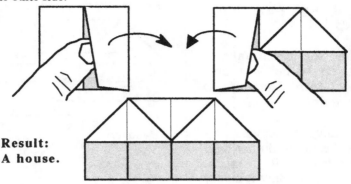

**Result: A house.**

She decided to leave her **house** *(demonstrate with Step #4)* and go to the music store to buy something new.

There was a clearance table in the far back corner of the store where everything was marked down to just twenty-five cents. A piano solo that had three different sections was right on top.

Mrs. Ivory studied the **first** part, then the **second**, and finally the **third**.

*(Fold the three parts of Step #5 as you say each word.)*

**Step #5:** Fold the front flap up three times along the dotted lines. The bottom of the third fold should be level with the edge of the rooftop formed in the last step. Each fold represents a different section of music.

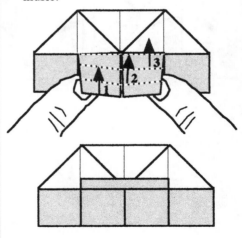

**Result: The three sections of music.**

The music was unusual and a little difficult to play, but she decided to let the clerk **wrap it up**, *(demonstrate with Step #6)*

...so that she could take it home to try on her very own **piano**. *(Open Step #6 to reveal the finished piano.)*

The new music was perfect for the fancy dinner, and Mrs. Ivory liked it so much, she continued to play it nearly every day.

**Step #6:** Fold each side to the middle along the dotted lines to simulate the wrapping.

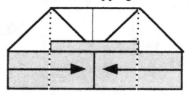

**Result: The wrapped package.**

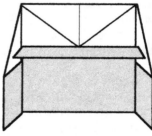

Swing each side open and let the keyboard fall forward to jut out a bit.

**The complete piano.**

# Optional Follow-Up Activities

1. This traditional origami piano can be constructed from rectangles of any size or dimension, including squares, as in this story. Try folding another piano with a different size piece of paper, making sure to label each step with its name from the story. Pairing the story events with the folding steps greatly enhances short-term memory of both. Don't be surprised when rectangles produce pianos with different dimensions. The height of the piano is determined by the first fold in Step #1. Try folding one along its 8.5″ midline and another along it's 11″ midline. Compare the results.

2. The house formed in Step #4 will stand without support by simply mountain folding along the dotted lines and positioning as shown below:

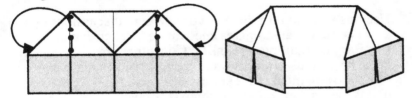

3. Make an ornamental box (or crown) from the same mountain fold. Instead of positioning as a house, lay the figure flat. (This box must be constructed from a square.)

Fold up the corners of the top layer.

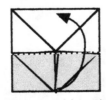

Fold the resulting triangle up to the top edge.

Repeat on the reverse side.

Insert both hands and open the figure so that the top collapses inwardly.

Square the sides by pinching the midline of each point. Invert the figure.

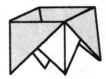

**The complete ornamental box.**

4. Draw the black and white piano keys onto the keyboard, ask for predictions about where they are located on the original square, and then completely unfold to discover the answer. Refold and observe the decorations reappear in their intended positions.

5. This figure can function as a shelf to display other origami models or as a miniature writing desk in a doll house. Simply modify the width of Step #5 to achieve the desired shape.

6. Imagine what it would be like to take piano lessons from Mrs. Ivory. Write a scene from a lesson. Include a description of her and her studio. Compare and contrast the results. Discuss how everyone who hears a story visualizes its physical elements differently.

7. Use this story to introduce or complement discussions about:
   a. The financial struggles encountered by musicians.
   b. Bargain hunting. Frugality. Consumerism.
   c. The various subjective and tangible values inherent in choosing music for certain occasions.
   d. What type of music has three sections?
   e. How many people are negatively impacted when bills aren't paid?
   f. Would Mrs. Ivory be frugal even if she had more money? Why or why not?

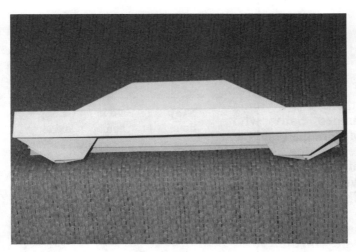

Learn inside reverse folding the easy way with this flashy car.

**About the story:** A young woman dreams of sailing around the world, but needs to win a contest to make her dream come true.

**Recommended ages:**
Listening only: All ages.
Listening & paperfolding: age 7 - adult.

**Required materials:** A large rectangle prefolded into the car and then completely unfolded for storytelling.

**Special notes:**
1. In Step #2, make sure the points of the two corners end up an equal distance from the lower edge.

2. In Step #3, opening the figure a bit will help in pushing the corner to the inside. Use the creases made in Step #2 to force the inside reverse fold to collapse along established fold lines.

A DREAM COME TRUE

# A Dream Come True

Once there was a young woman named Sally who dreamed of sailing around the world. She had the time to go, but unfortunately, she didn't have a boat or any money. Then one day she picked up a **brochure** that looked something like this. *(Demonstrate with Step #1.)*

It described a contest for the most original boat ever made. The rules said that the boat had to be large enough for two people, have space to store cargo, and be totally different from any boat ever invented before.

The first prize was $50,000 in cash and a fully equipped 30´ yacht. This was exactly what Sally needed to make her dream come true, so she went right to work.

Most boats have upright sails placed near the center, but Sally thought that if she was going to make an original design, she should try to put the sails somewhere else, like maybe on the corners, like this. *(Demonstrate with Step #2.)*

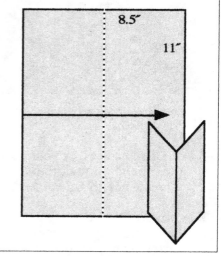

**Step #1:** Fold in half along the dotted line. Then open and close to simulate a brochure.

8.5˝
11˝

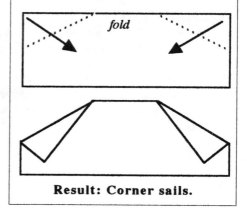

**Step #2:** Position the figure with the folded edge on top. Fold down the corners as shown below.

*fold*

**Result: Corner sails.**

When she tested the sails in the wind, they **collapsed**, *(demonstrate with Step #3)* which turned out to be a perfect solution for the **bottom** of the boat. *(Turn the figure upside down.)*

But then the sides were too high, so she **shortened** them like this. *(Demonstrate with Step #4.)*

Now there was room for two people and a space for cargo in between, just like the rules required. *(Point to the two triangles to represent people and the pocket between them as the storage space.)*

But when Sally tried her boat in the water, it was much too tippy. She decided to make it safer by adding an **extra float** to each side, like this. *(Demonstrate with Step #5.)*

**Step #3:** Unfold the corners and push them inside the figure to create pockets which represent collapsed sails.

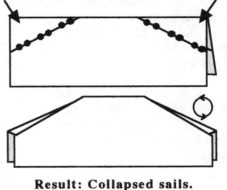

**Result: Collapsed sails.**

**Step #4:** Fold the top edge down to meet the bottom edge. Repeat on the reverse side.

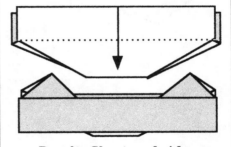

**Result: Shortened sides.**

**Step #5:** Fold the bottom edge up to the top edge along the dotted line as shown. Repeat on the reverse side.

**Result: Extra floats are added to the sides.**

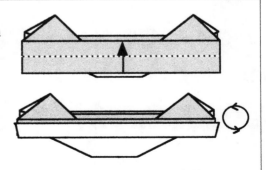

The boat worked great, but the extra special feature that Sally knew would make her's a winning design was what happened to it when it was out of the water. *(Invert the model and round out both tires as in Step #6.)*

You just flip it over and drive away. And that's exactly what she planned to do as soon as her prizes arrived.

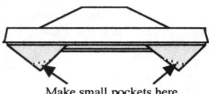

**Step #6:** Round out the tires by pushing these corners to the inside of the figure.

Make small pockets here.

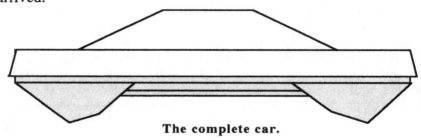

**The complete car.**

# Optional Follow-Up Activities

1. This easy origami car can be constructed from rectangles of any size or dimension, including squares. Try folding another car with a different size piece of paper, making sure to label each step with its name from the story. Pairing the story events with the folding steps greatly enhances short-term memory of both. Don't be surprised when individual folders produce cars with slightly different dimensions. The shape of the car is determined by the shape of the corner sails in Step #2.

2. Try modifying the corner folds in Step #2, leaving all other procedures unchanged. For example, the following changes will result in a sleek sports car:

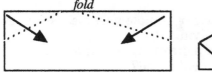 

Be careful to fold the corners down the same distance. These corners become the tires in the final step. The car is out of balance if one of the tires hangs down lower than the other.

3. Add body details and front headlights by modifying the car as follows:

Fold down the outer layer here. Repeat on the reverse side.

Push this corner to the inside of the figure to create a headlight. Repeat on the reverse side.

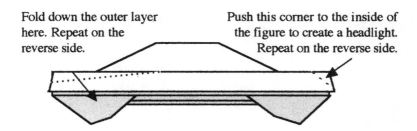

4. Use paper that's white on one side and colored on the other for maximum contrasts. Most traditional origami paper is already prepackaged like this. Create your own special effects by painting or texturizing one side of regular copy paper. Position the decorated side face down in Step #1. Gray represents the undecorated side.

5. Sponsor a contest for your classroom or organization. Ask the students to create the entry blanks, think of the prizes, write the rules, determine criteria for winners, and select the judges. Require participation or make it voluntary by awarding bonus points for entering.

6. What adventures might Sally encounter on her trip around the world? Will she travel alone? Will she run out of money? Are there dangers? Write a short story or play about what happens to her after she wins first prize.

7. Research how to fold origami boats. Most are simple to fold and are included in several books shelved in the 736 section (Dewey decimal system) of public libraries. Use the boats and cars to illustrate your own stories about Sally.

8. Use this story to introduce or complement discussions about:
   a. Creative problem solving.
   b. How it feels to have a dream. Goal setting.
   c. Buoyancy. How is it enhanced?
   d. Possible routes across land and sea.

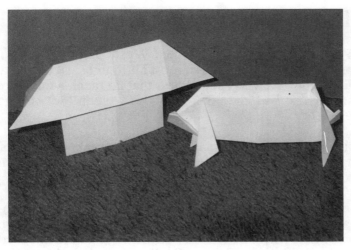

Fold the cabin in 5 easy steps, then continue on to make a pig.

**About the story:** A shunned cowboy builds a new home in the wilderness. End the story with a simple origami cabin or choose the second ending to transform the cabin into a pig.

**Recommended ages:**
Listening only: All ages.
Listening & paperfolding: age 7 - adult.

**Required materials:** A large square prefolded into the cabin (or pig) and then completely unfolded for storytelling. You must decide which ending you're using before starting the story. If you choose Ending #2, skip the first option. Don't say it at all.

**Special notes:**
1. It's very important to flip the model over before folding Step #3.

2. Steps #5 and #6 are much easier when a thumb is inserted between the layers of paper.

THE LEGEND OF WYATT BURP

# The Legend Of Wyatt Burp

About 150 years ago, a cowboy named Wyatt Burp was known far and wide as the sloppiest, clumsiest, most all-thumbsiest cowpoke west of the Mississippi. He was such a mess that no ranch would hire him, and he smelled so bad, the other cowboys wouldn't let him go on cattle drives, either.

They'd plug their noses and snarl, "Would you take a whiff of that tangled up heap of fleas and knees? Ole Wyatt Burp is worse'n pig puke, snake spit, and yesterday's beans all rolled into one."

For a clumsy, smelly guy, Wyatt Burp was thin-skinned, too. He got mad and took off for the unclaimed wilderness, hoping to make a life for himself where he could be as messy as nature intended him to be. He traveled a long way and finally reached a wide, **deep river** *(demonstrate with Step #1)* that he built a **long bridge** across, like this. *(Demonstrate with Step #2.)*

---

**Step #1:** Fold in half along the dotted line. Then open slightly to simulate a deep river.

**Result: A deep river.**

**Step #2:** Open Step #1 and fold the top and bottom sides to the middle along the dotted lines, opening slightly to simulate a long bridge.

**Result: A long bridge.**

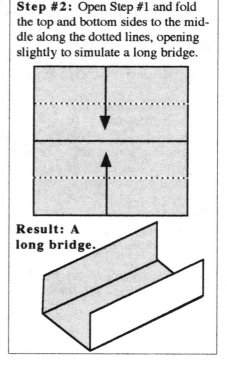

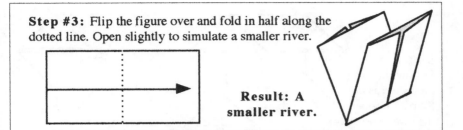

**Step #3:** Flip the figure over and fold in half along the dotted line. Open slightly to simulate a smaller river.

**Result: A smaller river.**

Then he crossed a few **smaller rivers** *(demonstrate with Step #3)* by building **shorter bridges**, like this. *(Demonstrate with Step #4.)*

Finally he reached a flat section of land *(flatten Step #4)* that had lots of wild game, clean water, and a nice shady spot for a messy **little cabin**, that looked like this. *(Demonstrate with Step #5.)*

**Ending #1:** He lived here for the rest of his life and was never compared to pig puke, snake spit, or yesterday's beans again.

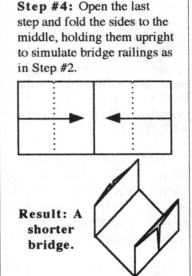

**Step #4:** Open the last step and fold the sides to the middle, holding them upright to simulate bridge railings as in Step #2.

**Result: A shorter bridge.**

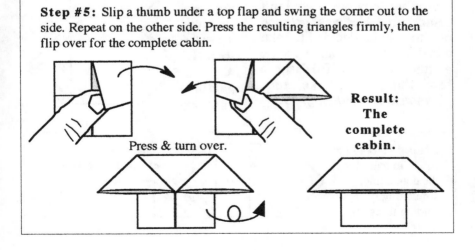

**Step #5:** Slip a thumb under a top flap and swing the corner out to the side. Repeat on the other side. Press the resulting triangles firmly, then flip over for the complete cabin.

Press & turn over.

**Result: The complete cabin.**

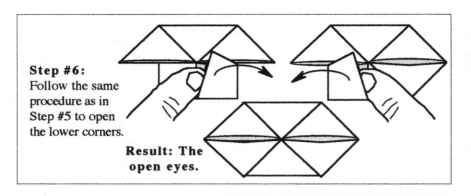

**Step #6:** Follow the same procedure as in Step #5 to open the lower corners.

**Result: The open eyes.**

**Ending #2:** At first, Wyatt was afraid of grizzly bears and rattle snakes, so he kept both **eyes** open all the time, like this. *(Demonstrate with Step #6.)*

Eventually he relaxed and let **one eye close** at night *(demonstrate with Step #7)* but his other eye stayed **partly open**, just in case... *(Demonstrate with Step #8.)*

It wasn't long before Ole Wyatt Burp caught on to why the other cowboys couldn't stand him. He was grossed out, too, so he decided to take a bath once a year and become a little neater by **folding** a few things up, like this. *(Demonstrate with Step #9.)*

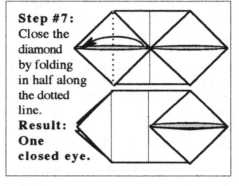

**Step #7:** Close the diamond by folding in half along the dotted line.

**Result: One closed eye.**

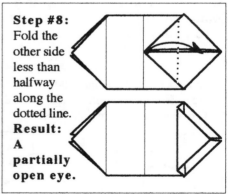

**Step #8:** Fold the other side less than halfway along the dotted line.

**Result: A partially open eye.**

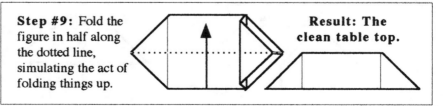

**Step #9:** Fold the figure in half along the dotted line, simulating the act of folding things up.

**Result: The clean table top.**

And then he discovered all the amazing things he could do on the surface of a clean table... *(point to the table top resulting from Step #9)* ...if he repaired the **four table legs**, that is.

*(Demonstrate with Step #10.)*

Hot diggidy, there was no stopping him, now! He went into a cleaning frenzy, putting things away in the **front** of the cabin and putting things away in the **rear** of the cabin, too.

*(Demonstrate with Step #11. The "front" is the snout and the "rear" is the tail.)*

Yes siree, by the time other settlers moved in, Ole Wyatt Burp wasn't nearly the **pig** *(finish adjusting the snout and hold up the finished pig)* he used to be, but he wasn't a cowboy anymore, either.

He'd become a farmer. A pig farmer. And a mighty root'n toot'n one at that.

**Step #10:** Slip a thumb under the left flap and swing the corner over to the right, then fold the edge back to the middle as shown. The back leg is already in position to be folded in half. Repeat on the reverse side.

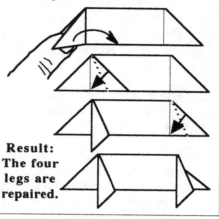

**Result: The four legs are repaired.**

**Step #11:** Fold the snout and tail up as shown. Then square off the snout by bending the point to the back.

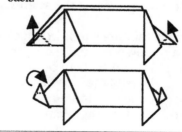

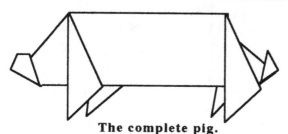

**The complete pig.**

# Optional Follow-Up Activities

1. Make more cabins or pigs with smaller squares, making sure to label each step with its name from the story. Pairing story events with folding steps greatly enhances short-term memory of both, and using ever smaller paper decreases rushing and increases precision.

2. Draw details like shingles or spots on the finished models. Predict where your markings will be when unfolded. Were you right? Refold and note when the markings return to final locations.

3. Use the cabins as name tags, ornaments, place marks, or lace with yarn for necklaces. This simple house is also useful as a prop for puppet shows.

4. Make a family of pigs, using 3″ squares for piglets. Experiment with different paper textures, such as aluminum foil, construction paper, waxed paper, freezer wrap, paper grocery bags, gift wrap, or wallpaper. Avoid tissue papers or plastics that do not retain creases.

5. List the exaggerations found throughout this tall tale. Then write your own with original characters and settings. Staple origami models onto final drafts for three-dimensional illustrations. Present the stories at your own Tall Tale Festival.

6. Use this story to introduce or complement discussions about:
   a. Cowboys and the Wild West.
   b. How it feels to be shunned.
   c. Possible reasons for choosing to be disorganized or poorly groomed.
   d. Pig farming. Annual sales? Annual consumption of pork?
   e. Liars contests or festivals.
   f. Traditional tall tales set in the American West.

# For More Information...

**National Organizations:** The following groups provide newsletters, web sites, and listings for regional groups. They also sponsor special events and distribute books and supplies. Membership is easily obtained online by entering them in Internet search engines or by inquiring at the addresses listed below:

**National Storytelling Network**
101 Courthouse Square
Jonesborough, TN 37659

**Origami USA**
15 West 77th Street
New York, NY 10024-5192

## Books that combine stories and origami:

■ Kallevig, Christine Petrell, 1993, *All About Pockets: Storytime Activities for Early Childhood*, p. 40, Broadview Hts., OH: Storytime Ink Intl.

■ Kallevig, Christine Petrell, 1993, *Bible Folding Stories: Old Testament Stories and Paperfolding Together As One*, Broadview Hts., OH: Storytime Ink Intl.

■ Kallevig, Christine Petrell, 1991, *Folding Stories: Storytelling and Origami Together As One*, Broadview Hts., OH: Storytime Ink Intl.

■ Kallevig, Christine Petrell, 1992, *Holiday Folding Stories: Storytelling and Origami Together For Holiday Fun*, Broadview Hts., OH: Storytime Ink Intl.

■ Murry and Rigney, 1928, *Paper Folding For Beginners,* Dover.

■ Pellowski, Anne, 1987, *Family Storytelling Handbook,* p. 74-84 (two stories written by Gay Merrill Gross), New York, NY: Macmillan Publishing Co.

■ Rey, H. A., 1952, *Curious George Rides A Bike,* New York, NY: Houghton.

■ Schimmel, Nancy, 1982, *Just Enough To Make A Story: A Sourcebook For Storytellers,* p. 20-32, Berkeley, CA: Sisters' Choice Press.

# Index

The author, Christine Petrell Kallevig, is available to tell stories or present educational workshops at schools, conferences, conventions, festivals, or other gatherings. For details, contact the publisher, Storytime Ink International, at (440) 838-4881 or write to P. O. Box 470505, Cleveland, Ohio 44147.

Use this coupon to order additional copies of **Fold-Along Stories** (**ISBN 0-9628769-9-2 $11.50**) or any of the other popular books published by Storytime Ink International. *(Library patrons – please photocopy.)*

**All About Pockets: Storytime Activities for Early Childhood** - The ultimate guide for how to use simple pockets as fun and effective educational tools. 128 pages of pocket poems, fingerplays, games, stories (includes one folding story), songs, riddles, and crafts. All activities emphasize the important eye-ear-hand-body connectedness that defines the intellectual, social, and emotional growth of young children. Easy to use, fun for kids age 3-7, and a perfect companion to storytelling aprons. Recommended for preschool teachers, storytellers, librarians, and day care providers. ISBN 0-9628769-6-8 $9.95

**Holiday Folding Stories: Storytelling and Origami Together For Holiday Fun** - 9 short stories illustrated by 9 easy origami models for ages 4 - adult. Stories for Columbus Day, Halloween, Thanksgiving, Hanukkah, Christmas, Valentine's Day, Easter, May Day, and Mother's Day. Includes holiday facts, optional activities, complete illustrated instructions, index, and photographs. ISBN 0-9628769-1-7 $11.50

**Bible Folding Stories: Old Testament Stories and Paperfolding Together As One** - Includes The 23rd Psalm, Jacob's ladder, Jonah's big fish, Noah's dove, Moses' basket, Ruth & Naomi's spike of wheat, Joseph's robe, Elijah's jar of oil, & Sarah's baby. Complete illustrated directions, photographs, and optional activities. Recommended for all ages and all Judeo-Christian faiths. ISBN 0-9628769-4-1 $11.50

**Ticklish Tales for Tellers: 99 Jokes & Riddles About Storytellers** - 32 pages of very short stories, cartoons, and jokes lampooning storytellers and the challenges they face during performances. Recommended as a gag gift for amateur and professional tellers. ISBN 0-9628769-5-X $4.99

name _____
address _____

city/state _____
zip code _____

Please send me:

| Qty. | ISBN number | Price | Total |
|------|-------------|-------|-------|
|      |             |       |       |
|      |             |       |       |
|      |             |       |       |
|      | SUBTOTAL    |       |       |
| Ohio residents add 7% sales tax | | | |
| Postage & handling: Add $2 (1st book), $1 @ additional book | | | |
| **US dollars only** TOTAL ENCLOSED | | | |

Write checks to:
Storytime Ink International
Mail to:
Storytime Ink International
P. O. Box 470505
Cleveland, OH 44147-0505

Allow 2 weeks for delivery.